Letters
From
Bethlehem

Five Dramatic Monologues
For Advent

Wayne L. Tilden

CSS Publishing Company, Inc., Lima, Ohio

LETTERS FROM BETHLEHEM

Reprinted 2002

For more information about CSS Publishing Company resources, visit our website at www.csspub.com or e-mail us at custserv@csspub.com or call (800) 241-4056.

ISBN 0-7880-1027-1

To Dick, who gave me the inspiration for these monologues; and to Kathryn, Brian, Molly, and Fred, who brought them to life originally.

Letters from Bethlehem

Notes

These vignettes may be memorized or may be presented in "modified Readers' Theatre" format — the actor actually reading the letter aloud as it is being "written." Each selection is followed by a suggested song. This is, however, just that — a suggestion. Please feel free to use your own creativity in selecting these musical numbers for your choir or congregation.

Costuming

Costuming should be biblical or suggestive of the biblical time period. Each actor should match the suggested characterization below.

Angel — Dressed in white.

Shepherd — Dressed in rustic "earth tones," possibly somewhat "down at the heel," but clean.

Wise Man — Dressed royally; lots of reds, purples, perhaps a crown, and lots of jewelry.

Mary — Dressed simply. A "homespun" look. Perhaps the traditional blue, but be creative. Her hair should be covered.

Christ — Costume is more suggestive than accurately biblical. You may want to experiment with this one, based on your actor and his abilities.

The Angel

Locale: *Somewhere outside of time and space. The letter is addressed "generally."*

"My Friend,

"Delivering Good News is always a joyous event. Therefore, when it befell me to deliver, that night, what would be the gladdest of tidings to 'all people upon whom his favor rests,' I was highly honored.

"To be chosen from the whole Host of our Company for this privilege has been the most memorable experience of my life. And to see the fulfillment of the Promise laid down in ages past has brought a feeling of Glory to my innermost Being.

"As we Messengers continued the proclamation of the Good News of the birth of a Savior to all humankind, and as we sang out in our multitudes, 'Glory to God in the highest, and on earth peace and goodwill toward mankind,' I felt something stir within me which I had never felt before.

"The promise of a Messiah, 'the Desire of the Ages,' had come. I have been able to see the response of humanity to a Promise from the beginning of Time. Hopefully, that response will continue to be reflected in the faces of all, down through the ages, who hear the continued proclamation of that Gospel; 'Joy to the World: the Lord is come!'

"Peace,

"Gabriel"

Suggested song: "Joy To The World"

7

The Shepherd

Locale: *On a hill, outside of Bethlehem — the next morning.*

"Dear family,

"I doubt if I can make you believe what happened to me, but if I don't tell somebody I'm gonna bust. It was the most ... astounding ... thing you ever saw!

"Last night me and the fellahs was watchin' the sheep, jus' like always, when all of a sudden the sky lit up and there was this voice. Well, we was scared near to death. But the voice says, 'Fear not!' it says. Then we looks up and there is this ... being ... in glowing white clothes. (It turned out that he was an angel from heaven!)

"The angel went on: 'Behold, I bring you Good News of a great joy which is coming to *everybody.* A Savior, who is *Messiah Elohim,* is born this very night. The proof of this prophecy is this — *you* will find the baby wrapped up in cloths and lying in the manger of Bethlehem.'

"Well, we didn't hardly take time to talk over what to do next. We got up quick, and went and found the baby with his parents, just like the angel said we would. After we had paid our respects to the baby and his mom and dad, we went back to our work in the hills.

"So, I been thinkin' ever since — if this really was our Messiah, our Savior, how come *Yahweh* God sent his angel from heaven to tell *us* — just plain, simple country folks? Why not the priests and the rabbis? Who are *we* gonna tell?

"But it was such a pretty sight. That sweet, sweet baby jus' lyin' there, lookin' quietly up at me like I was somebody special. And his mother. Those proud, young eyes — lookin' at her baby as though she knew somethin' about him that nobody else did. I can't explain it, but it made me feel real special — like I'd become part of something that had never happened before. I just wish *everyone* could have experienced that 'silent night,' that 'heavenly peace.'

"Your son,

"Shaul"

Suggested song: "Silent Night, Holy Night"

The Wise Man

Locale: *In his tent on the return trip.*

"To my lord and to his lady; to the members of the court and to the ladies of the household: 'Greetings!'

"My quest, and the Object upon which my associates and I set out, has reached its completion and I will soon be back in your presence.

"While the quest itself was arduous, never was there complaint. We knew for Whom we sought and that assuaged our fatigue and our fears. While great reaches of our way were unknown to us, we knew, my lord, that our Object would make the trip worth any of its negative aspects.

"We had hoped that finding a newborn king of the Jews would be occasioned by soliciting information from the current ruler, but in that aspect we erred. Rather, even his seers and holy men were surprised and taken aback to inform us that this new king was to be born in the nearby village of '*Bet-l'Hem.*'

"King Herod, for that is the name of his Judeo-Aramean pretender to the throne, commanded that we should search for this young child and then inform him as to the Child's whereabouts — so that he also might honor the new King.

"We did, indeed, find the Child where he was staying with his parents in a small house in that same small village. We left our gifts for the young Prince — gold, for his royalty; incense, for his deity; and myrrh, for his atoning death.

"Before we returned to '*Yeru-Shalem,*' however, we were warned by the Jewish God not to return by that way because Herod had it in his mind to harm the Child.

"I am unable to imagine a mind so cruel and malignant as to desire to harm a child out of his own vindictiveness. If only he had been able to truly worship, as we had, I am sure that then he, too,

10

would realize and understand what a wonderful Gift to all human-kind is this little Savior-King. He has come to *all* of us, Jew and Gentile, male and female, to be the 'perfect light,' the 'Light of the World.'

"Your loyal subject,

"Gaspar"

Suggested song: "We Three Kings"

Mary

Locale: *A room in the home of Mary and Joseph in Bethlehem — shortly after the Census.*

"Dear Mama,

"At last I'm finding the time to tell you of all that has happened since we left '*Naz-a'Ret*' those oh-so-many weeks ago.

"The roads were so, so crowded as we journeyed up here to '*Bet-l'Hem.*' The dusty roads and my advanced pregnancy just made the whole trip so much more tiring.

"When we finally got here, it was late and the inn was full. But when Joseph told the man that I was just about to give birth, he let us have some hay and a manger trough in a corner of the stable, amidst the warmth of the livestock.

"While we were there, Mama, some shepherds from out in the hills came and told us that *angels* had told them of my little Jesus' being born that night. Imagine, Mama, angels taking notice of my little baby.

"And just the other day some astrologers from Mesopotamia came and *worshiped* my baby and brought him expensive gifts — gold, frankincense, and myrrh.

"Oh, Mama, my heart is ready to burst! To be selected by God as 'highly favored among women.' To be chosen to bear and to raise his Son. And to know, as no one else can know, that this little Son of mine will one day bring 'peace on earth, and mercy mild.'

"Oh, Mama, I only hope and pray that *all* people might someday remember what a special little baby this Child of mine is, and that, somehow, it might affect their lives in a profound way.

"Your loving daughter,

"Mary"

Suggested song: "What Child Is This?"

Christ

Locale: *The same as in "The Angel," outside of time and space.*

"My dear little children,

"At this time of year I AM reminded of how we all show our Love for one another. I AM encouraged as I see my people come together like this to worship and to remember the true meaning of this Celebration.

"Sometimes, though, my little ones, my heart breaks for each one of you. I have done so much for you and yet I see so little of what I offered in Love being returned — even among yourselves.

"The angels of heaven recognized that I AM the Promised One on that evening so long ago, and they could not restrain the Joy that they felt. They sang it in Love from the heavens, and it echoed from the mountainsides.

"When the shepherds heard it, they understood that I AM the Lamb of God. They left their flocks on the hillsides and came in Love, showing their desire to experience who I AM, even at the risk of their livelihood.

"Wise men — astrologers — from far-off Mesopotamia saw prophecy of my existence and came in Love and at great expense of life and limb to express their adoration and joy at the birth of the new King — the Light of the World.

"My mother Mary, risking shame, brought me into this world, little understanding what it meant to bear the Messiah, but Loving me as her own, and because I AM the Way.

"Now, my beloved, I invite you to recognize, at this season, who I AM. I AM the savior of humankind and I AM desirous of a personal relationship with you. 'Come unto me all of you who labor' and are burdened with the cares of the day. I AM able to lift that burden from you because I Love you!

"I AM, your Loving Savior,

"Jesus Christ"

Suggested song: "Come, Thou Long-Expected Jesus"

www.ingramcontent.com/pod-product-compliance
Lightning Source LLC
Chambersburg PA
CBHW071814020426
42331CB00009B/2496